THE KARACHI KITCHEN

THE KARACHI KITCHEN

CLASSIC *and* CONTEMPORARY FLAVORS *of* PAKISTAN

KAUSAR AHMED

*Photography by David Broder
and Maryam Ashraf*

THE KARACHI KITCHEN © copyright 2017 by Kausar Ahmed. All rights reserved. No part of this book may be reproduced in any form whatsoever, by photography or xerography or by any other means, by broadcast or transmission, by translation into any kind of language, nor by recording electronically or otherwise, without permission in writing from the author, except by a reviewer, who may quote brief passages in critical articles or reviews.

ISBN 13: 978-1-63489-095-3

Library of Congress Catalog Number: 2017954661
Printed in the United States of America
First Printing: 2017

21 20 19 18 17   5 4 3 2 1
Design by Joyce Hwang

Wise Ink Creative Publishing replaces every tree used in printing their books by planting thousands of trees every year in reforestation programs. Learn more at **wiseinkpub.com**.

WISE Ink
CREATIVE PUBLISHING

837 Glenwood Avenue
Minneapolis, MN 55405

To order, visit **thekarachikitchen.com**. Reseller discounts available.

DEDICATION

This book is dedicated to the two most important chapters of my life and the key people in them: my parents and my children.

Growing up around parents who dedicated their life's work to equal education for girls in Pakistan, I grew up to be an adventurous go-getter. My parents taught me how to empathize; be patient, kind, and strong; and never give up. They taught me to work hard, and it is their love and prayers that have led me to success each day of my life.

My three children have taught me to be patient, loving, daring, caring, furious, perplexed, strong, and joyful. Their love for food inspired me to master (and sometimes re-appropriate) my mother's recipes and experiment with new textures and flavors. My children are my pillars of support—my guides who have shown me the beauty of life and reminded me to believe in myself.

CONTENTS

To the Reader   *viii*

TOPPINGS AND SAUCES

Green Coconut Chutney	1
Sweet and Spicy Plum Chutney	2
Masala (Spice Blend)	4
Tamarind and Mint Chutney	9
Tamarind and Date Chutney	7
Raita (Yogurt Sauce)	8

SIDES AND SNACKS

Achar (Carrot Pickle)	13
Fried Okra Chips	15
Aaloo Chat (Potato Salad)	17
Namak Paray (Pastry Ribbons)	19
Spiced Orange Salad	21
Bun Kabab (Potato Burger) with Green Coconut Chutney	27
Dahi Bare (Dumplings in Yogurt)	25
Stuffed Green Pepper Pakoras (Fritters)	27

MAIN COURSES

Dum Kay Pasanday (Masala-Rubbed Roast Beef Tenderloin)	33
Kofte (Meatball Curry)	35
Murgh Hara Masala (Green Chicken)	39
Masala Fish	41
Daal (Lentil Curry)	43
Shaami Kabab	45
Chicken Crepes	47
Kausari Rice	51
Mutton Do Piaza (Lamb Stew)	53
Lentil and Rice Pilaf	55
Khao Suey (Coconut Noodle Soup)	57

DESSERTS

Nan Khatai (Shortbread Biscuit)	63
Fruit Trifle	65
Gajar Ka Halwa (Carrot Delight)	67
Pineapple Soufflé	71
Vanilla Saffron Cheesecake	73
Apple Pie	75
Black Forest Cake	79
Shahi Tukray (Bread Pudding)	81

Acknowledgments	*85*
About the Author	*86*
Index	*89*

TO THE READER

Dear reader,

Thank you for picking up my cookbook. Within these pages, I've included my beloved recipes from Pakistan and the surrounding region that are close to my heart. I believe food connects people, and I invite you to use the recipes in this book to connect and celebrate with the important people in your life.

I was born and raised in a traditional Pakistani home, and my life has been a joyful, vibrant, and diverse culinary journey. I grew up in Karachi, a bustling port city at the mouth of the Arabian Sea that is as abundant in history as it is in culinary diversity. Fishing villages along what is now the Karachi coast sprang up thousands of years ago and have served as a hub through recent centuries for local tribes as well as the British, Turks, Mughals, and Arabs, to name a few. Regional cuisine in Karachi is a hybrid of South Asian, Central Asian, Middle Eastern, and European ingredients and styles of preparation. Dishes range from mild to spicy, are strong in flavor, and come in a variety of forms, including curries, stews, soups, sandwiches, wraps, and pilafs.

While I was growing up, dinner was always a communal event—the entire family gathered together and my mother prepared the meal with enthusiasm. We frequently had visitors—grandparents, aunts and uncles, cousins, neighbors, friends, or my father's business associates who were visiting from overseas. Eating meals together was an essential part of our daily routine. Warm aromas would float out of the kitchen and cause a sensory explosion that would draw my brothers and me to the dinner table. A well-rounded spread featuring freshly prepared local ingredients would welcome us. Meats and vegetables were cooked to perfection with ground and whole spices, such as cardamom, pepper, cumin, and clove, always accompanied by a side of salad, rice, and fresh homemade *roti* (flatbread).

As I grew older and started helping my mother with meals, my love for cooking grew and turned into a therapeutic activity for me. It wasn't just the process of cooking that I loved—cooking for my loved ones and bringing people together at the dinner table gave me immense pleasure. Cooking brought me closer to my community and evolved into a passion that eventually became a career.

For this book I have compiled traditional and contemporary Pakistani recipes, which are deeply connected to my childhood and, later, motherhood. I hope these recipes bring you joy, curiosity, and adventure.

Flavorfully,

Kausar

Photograph by Farah Abed

TOPPINGS and SAUCES

GREEN COCONUT CHUTNEY

Delicious with kababs and fritters or in sandwiches, you can also try this recipe with the *Lentil and Rice Pilaf* or *Shaami Kabab* recipes.

Active time: *10 minutes* | **Total time:** *10 minutes*

- ½ cup fresh or dry coconut, grated
- 2 garlic cloves
- 2 green chilies
- ½ cup cilantro leaves, chopped
- ½ cup mint leaves
- 1 teaspoon lemon juice
- 4 tablespoons water
- ¼ teaspoon salt

- Place all ingredients in a food processor and grind to a paste. Serve immediately or refrigerate in an airtight container for up to 2 weeks.

SWEET *and* SPICY PLUM CHUTNEY

Try this unique chutney as a topping for the *Lentil and Rice Pilaf* and *Masala Fish*.

Active time: 10 minutes | *Total time: 1 hour 10 minutes*

- 2 cups dried plums
- 2 cups water
- ¼ cup white vinegar
- ½ cup brown sugar
- 1 tablespoon melon seeds
- ¼ teaspoon chili powder
- ½ teaspoon red chili flakes
- ½ teaspoon salt
- 1 teaspoon yellow mustard seeds
- 1 2-inch cinnamon stick

- **In large stainless steel or enameled pan, add the plums, water, vinegar, sugar, melon seeds, chili powder, red chili flakes, salt, yellow mustard seeds, and cinnamon stick. Bring to a boil, turn down the heat, and leave to simmer for an hour, giving the occasional stir to reduce the risk of the chutney sticking. Cook until chutney reaches desired thickness and cool. Remove the cinnamon stick. Spoon into jars and refrigerate for up to 3 weeks.**

MASALA
(Spice Blend)

This easy-to-make spice blend can be stored in a cool, dry place for several weeks. Use it for salads by mixing it with vinegar, olive oil, and a little bit of brown sugar to give it a spicy, sour, and sweet flavor, or season your favorite dishes with it. Sprinkle it over the *Spiced Orange Salad*, *Aaloo Chaat*, or *Dahi Bare* for extra flavor.

Active time: 10 minutes | **Total time:** 10 minutes

- ¾ teaspoon cumin seeds
- ½ teaspoon black peppercorns
- ¼ teaspoon curry powder
- ½ teaspoon chili powder
- ½ teaspoon salt
- ⅛ teaspoon ground cinnamon

- Dry-roast all ingredients on the stove on low heat for about 2 minutes, until light golden-brown. Cool and grind the mixture into a fine powder with a food processor. Store spice blend in a jar and keep in a cool, dry place. Use for cooking as needed.

TAMARIND *and* MINT CHUTNEY

This chutney is traditionally used as a dip for finger food. Also try it with the *Bun Kabab* or *Shaami Kabab*.

Active time: *10 minutes* | **Total time:** *10 minutes*

1 cup fresh mint leaves	2 to 3 green chilies	Salt, to taste
½ cup fresh cilantro leaves	¼ cup tamarind pulp	2 teaspoons brown sugar

- Combine all ingredients in a blender or food processor and purée well. Store in an airtight container for up to 1 week.

TAMARIND *and* DATE CHUTNEY

Traditionally used as a dip for fritters, this chutney can also be drizzled over the *Aaloo Chaat* or *Dahi Bare* along with some *Masala*.

Active time: 15 minutes | *Total time:* 1 hour 15 minutes

½ cup seedless dates
3 cups water, divided
½ cup tamarind paste
½ cup powdered jaggery* (can be replaced with brown sugar)
½ teaspoon cumin, ground and roasted
½ teaspoon chili powder
½ teaspoon salt
1 teaspoon chaat masala* (optional)

- Soak the dates in 1 cup water for 1 hour. In a food processor, grind the dates into a smooth paste. In a pan, add the tamarind paste, 2 cups water, jaggery (or brown sugar), cumin, chili powder, salt, and chaat masala (optional). Cook on low heat for 6 to 8 minutes or until thick. Add water if the chutney becomes too thick. Cool and store the tamarind and date chutney in an airtight jar in the refrigerator for up to 2 weeks.

*Jaggery and chaat masala can be found in most South Asian stores.

RAITA
(Yogurt Sauce)

Raita is traditionally eaten as a side with rice dishes but goes well with anything—bread, meat, vegetables, or as a topping on spicy dishes.

Active time: *20 minutes* | **Total time:** *20 minutes*

- 1 cup plain yogurt
- ¼ cup water
- ¼ teaspoon ground cumin
- ¼ teaspoon chili powder
- ¼ cup cucumber, peeled, seeded, and chopped
- ¼ cup red onion, finely chopped
- ¼ cup tomato, finely chopped
- ¼ cup cilantro, finely chopped
- ¼ teaspoon salt

- Mix yogurt and water together well. Add the spices, cucumber, onion, tomato, cilantro, and salt. Mix well and serve.

SIDES and SNACKS

ACHAR
(Carrot Pickle)

My paternal grandmother migrated to Karachi from Bombay during the partition of India and Pakistan. She always wore a long cotton dress and had us eat our meals on a tablecloth laid out on the floor. *Achar* was a staple on her menu and my favorite side. She would make it at home annually and store it all year round in huge clay jars. It can be served as a condiment with anything.

Active time: 1 hour | *Total time: 2 days* | *Serves 6–8*

- 3 medium-sized carrots, peeled and julienned
- 1½ teaspoons salt
- 1½ teaspoons mustard seeds, coarsely ground
- 1 teaspoon chili powder, or to taste
- ½ teaspoon turmeric
- ⅛ teaspoon asafetida powder* (optional)
- 1 tablespoon lemon juice
- 1 tablespoon mustard oil
- Green chili, sliced and seeded

- Wrap the julienned carrots in a dry towel, removing any excess water. Mix remaining ingredients together and put in a glass jar. Add carrots and cover jar. Set the jar in the sun for 24 hours. Refrigerate for up to 2 weeks.

---

* *Asafetida powder is found in Middle Eastern or South Asian stores.*

FRIED OKRA CHIPS

Served as a snack or a side dish at a dinner or lunch. For a burst of crunch and flavor, add a sprinkle of amchur (dry mango powder) and chili powder and a squeeze of lemon just before serving.

Active time: 20 minutes | *Total time: 1 hour* | *Serves 4–5*

- 1 pound okra (bhindi)
- 1 teaspoon ground allspice
- ¾ teaspoon amchur powder (dry mango powder)
- ¾ teaspoon chili powder
- Salt, to taste
- Oil for deep-frying
- 2 teaspoons lemon juice

- Rinse the okra in water. Wipe it dry with a kitchen napkin. Slice the okra vertically into 4 pieces. If you have small-sized okra, slice into 2 pieces. Place all the sliced okra in a big bowl. Sprinkle half of the spice powders on the okra. Marinate the okra for 25 to 30 minutes or up to an hour.

- Heat enough oil for deep-frying on medium-high heat. Carefully drop in the okra in small portions until it turns golden-brown. Keep turning every 2 to 3 minutes to ensure the portions don't burn, for about 4 to 5 minutes to get the golden-brown color on medium-high heat. Continue to fry in batches and drain on a kitchen towel. Sprinkle with remaining spices and lemon juice and serve immediately.

AALOO CHAAT
(Potato Salad)

My mother had a dozen siblings, a few with whom I was very close. One of my aunts lived near Islamabad. We visited her every year on our way up to the Himalayas, where we spent the summertime. She and her husband both had a love for cooking, eating, and feeding, and we enjoyed not three meals but at least five meals a day with them. This *Aaloo Chaat* recipe brings back fond memories of our time spent together. My aunt served this dish in the evening with tea and fritters, and she topped it with an assortment of chopped onions, tomatoes, green chilies, mint leaves, and cilantro.

Active time: 15 minutes | *Total time:* 30 minutes | *Serves* 2 3

- Salt, to taste
- 1 teaspoon ground coriander
- 4 to 5 dry whole red chilies
- ½ teaspoon cumin seeds
- 3 large potatoes, boiled, peeled, and cubed in ½ inch portions
- 1 tablespoon lemon juice
- 2 tablespoons tamarind paste
- 1 medium red onion, finely chopped
- 1 green chili, finely chopped
- ¼ cup fresh coriander leaves, chopped
- 8 to 10 mint leaves (mint leaves should be kept whole, as they change color if they are chopped)
- 20 tortilla chips, crushed

• Dry-roast salt, coriander, whole red chilies, and cumin seeds to make the spice powder. Let cool for 5 minutes, grind, and put aside. In a bowl, mix the potatoes, lemon juice, roasted spice powder, and tamarind paste. Mix well and transfer to a serving bowl. Garnish with onion, green chilies, coriander, and whole mint leaves. Add tortilla chips just before serving.

NAMAK PARAY
(Pastry Ribbons)

Namak Paray are traditional Pakistani ribbon-like pastry strips, delicately rolled out and cut into diamond shapes. Seasoned with cumin and carom seeds to give them extra flavor, these light and crispy chips are best served with tea. They can be stored in glass jars in a cool, dry place for several days.

Active time: 1 hour | *Total time: 1 hour* | *Serves 5–6*

- 2 cups flour
- ¼ teaspoon baking soda
- Salt, to taste
- 1 teaspoon carom seeds
- 1 teaspoon crushed black pepper
- 1 teaspoon cumin seeds
- 2 to 3 tablespoons oil or butter
- ½ to ¾ cup water
- 3 cups vegetable oil for deep-frying

- Sieve the flour, baking soda, and salt together. Add carom seeds, crushed black pepper, and cumin seeds. Add oil or butter. Gradually add water and knead to make a soft but firm dough.

- Roll out the dough into a thin rectangular or circular shape. With a knife or pastry cutter, make crisscross patterns on the dough to create diamond shapes. Remove the diamond-shaped patterns and keep aside on a lightly floured surface. Heat oil on medium-low. To test the readiness of the oil, drop in one ribbon to see if it rises to the surface; if it does, the oil is ready. In batches of 8 to 10, fry all the ribbons for 1 to 2 minutes on each side or until light golden-brown in color; use a wire skimmer to flip the ribbons as needed. Drain and cool on paper towel. The ribbons will become crisp as they cool. Once they have cooled, store in an airtight container for up to 2 weeks.

SPICED ORANGE SALAD

This spicy yet sweet version of orange salad is prepared with our homemade *Masala*. It's colorful, refreshing, and delicious. The sharpness of the onions almost immediately mellows down when combined with the oranges, and the flavors all seem to come together in perfect harmony. Try this salad with *Masala Fish* or *Shaami Kababs*. It's also an excellent accompaniment to hot stews or spiced dishes.

Active time: 20 minutes | *Total time: 20 minutes* | *Serves 6*

6 large oranges	1 teaspoon sugar	½ cup unsalted walnuts
4 to 6 tablespoons white vinegar	1 tablespoon (or to taste) Masala Spice Blend	½ cup fresh mint leaves, slivered
1 tablespoon olive oil	1 red onion, peeled and sliced into rings	

- With a small, sharp knife, cut, peel, and remove white membrane from oranges. Slice the oranges crosswise ⅛- to ¼-inch thick and discard seeds.

- To make the dressing, mix vinegar, olive oil, and sugar in a small bowl. Stir in the Masala Spice Blend and mix well.

- In a wide, shallow bowl, gently mix orange slices and onions. Pour in dressing and mix gently. Scatter walnuts and mint leaves. Spoon salad onto plates and serve with extra dressing.

BUN KABAB *with* GREEN COCONUT CHUTNEY
(Traditional Potato Burger)

My love affair with the *Bun Kabab* began when I was a child and was passed down to my children. Later, my son-in-law joined our family's addiction to this all-time favorite street food in Karachi. The *Bun Kabab* is best devoured with *Green Coconut Chutney*.

Active time: 1 hour | *Total time: 1 hour* | *Serves 4*

- 4 medium-sized potatoes
- ½ teaspoon chili flakes
- ½ teaspoon chili powder
- 1 teaspoon cumin seeds
- 1 teaspoon ground cumin
- ½ teaspoon ground allspice
- Salt, to taste
- 2 tablespoons lemon juice
- 1 medium-sized yellow onion, finely chopped
- ¼ cup cilantro, finely chopped
- 1 small green chili, finely chopped
- 2 eggs, beaten
- 4 burger buns
- 1 cucumber, sliced
- 1 medium onion, sliced into rings
- 1 medium tomato, sliced
- Butter lettuce leaves

- Boil, peel, and mash potatoes. Add chili flakes, chili powder, cumin seeds, cumin, allspice, salt, lemon juice, onion, cilantro, and green chili. Mix well. Divide the mixture into medium-sized balls and shape them into patties.

- Beat the eggs. Heat oil in a griddle to medium-high. Dip the patty in the egg and fry on both sides until slightly brown. Set aside. Toast the buns. Spread the Green Coconut Chutney on both sides. Place the cooked patties on the bun base. Top with cucumber, tomato, and lettuce leaf. Cover with bun top.

DAHI BARE
(Dumplings in Yogurt)

My mother's *Dahi Bare* became so popular in the family that my aunts would ask her to cater this dish for their dinners, lunches, or teas. This dish can be served with any meal, be it a brunch, lunch, tea, high tea, or dinner. Top it with a generous amount of *Tamarind and Date Chutney* and crunchy spicy chips or papri (found in Asian stores).

Active time: 1 hour | *Total time: 3 hours 30 minutes* | *Makes 15–18*

FOR THE BATTER

- 2 cups white maash daal (white lentils)
- 2 cups water (for soaking maash daal)
- ¼ teaspoon baking soda
- ½ teaspoon salt
- 3 cups vegetable oil (for frying)

FOR THE YOGURT SAUCE

- 3 cups plain yogurt
- ½ cup water
- ¼ teaspoon ginger paste
- ¼ teaspoon garlic paste
- 2 tablespoons sugar
- 1 tablespoon ground cumin
- ½ teaspoon chili powder

FOR THE CHILI TOPPING

- 2 tablespoons oil
- 4 to 5 dry whole red chilies
- 1 teaspoon cumin seeds
- 5 to 6 fresh curry leaves*
- ¼ cup fresh cilantro leaves, chopped

- Soak the lentils in water for at least 2 hours (up to 24). Drain the excess water completely. In the food processor, grind the lentils into a thick paste. Add the baking soda and salt; mix well and set aside for 30 minutes.

(continued)

---

*Fresh curry leaves are available at most South Asian stores.

- Heat oil in a deep pan on medium-high. Drop in a pea-sized ball to check if oil is hot. The oil should start sizzling, and the ball will gradually float up if oil is hot enough. Divide the batter into 1-inch balls, making about 15 to 18 patties. Shape each ball into a thick patty, around ¼ inch. Deep-fry patties for 3 to 4 minutes on each side until golden-brown. Drain on a paper towel.

- In a large bowl, whisk together the yogurt and water. Add ginger and garlic pastes, sugar, cumin, and chili powder; whisk well. Add fried patties in yogurt mixture.

- In a small pan, heat 2 tablespoons oil. Add whole red chilies, cumin seeds, and fresh curry leaves, and lightly fry for 1 minute. Pour chili mixture on yogurt. Cover and refrigerate for 1 hour. Garnish with cilantro and serve.

STUFFED GREEN PEPPER PAKORAS
(Fritters)

As the monsoon season begins in Karachi, fritters and tea will be served in every household at any time of the day to celebrate the much-awaited rainy season. Fritters can be served as an appetizer or on the side with rice and lentils. They also work well as a side for *Lentil and Rice Pilaf* served with *Raita*.

Active time: 20 minutes | *Total time: 20 minutes* | *Serves 6*

FOR TAMARIND STUFFING

- 4 tablespoons tamarind paste
- 2 teaspoons chili powder
- ¼ teaspoon salt
- ½ teaspoon ground cumin
- 1 teaspoon chaat masala* (optional)
- 1 teaspoon brown sugar
- 1 cup cream cheese (optional)

FOR THE CHILIES

- 6 to 8 green Anaheim chilies

FOR THE BATTER

- 2 cups gram flour (besan)
- ½ teaspoon baking soda
- 1 teaspoon chili powder
- ½ teaspoon cumin seeds
- 1 teaspoon salt
- 1½ cups of water, or as needed
- 3 cups of vegetable oil for deep-frying

- Mix tamarind paste, chili powder, salt, cumin, chaat masala (optional), brown sugar, and cream cheese (optional) in a bowl and set aside.

- Wash and pat dry the chilies. With a small, sharp knife, slit the chili lengthwise from the center just enough to deseed it and fill it. Remove

(continued)

---

* *Chaat masala is available at most South Asian stores.*

the seeds and rinse and dry chilies once more. Stuff the chilies with one heaped teaspoon of the spice and cream cheese mixture. Set aside.

- In a large bowl, mix the gram flour, baking soda, chili powder, cumin seeds, and salt. Gradually add the water, whisking constantly until it becomes a smooth, thick batter. Heat oil on high in a deep wok. To test the heat of the oil, drop in a pea-sized amount of the batter. Take one stuffed chili at a time and completely coat it by dipping it in the gram flour batter. Drop it in the hot oil. Drop in 2 to 3 chilies at a time.

- Turn the heat on medium-low. Let the fritters fry for 2 minutes before flipping them. Fry from all sides for 6 to 7 minutes or until golden-brown. Place fritters on a paper towel to absorb extra oil. Serve with *Green Coconut Chutney*.

MAIN COURSES

DUM KAY PASANDAY
(Masala-Rubbed Roast Beef Tenderloin)

My mother's side of the family migrated to Karachi from parts of Punjab and Uttar Pradesh in North India, bringing with them recipes, such as this one, which are very distinct in flavors and styles. In this tender and fragrant dry stew, a combination of spices works in concert with the heat of black peppercorns. I cannot find a better way of enjoying this dish than with piping hot naan, thinly sliced fresh onion, julienned ginger, and green chili. Given the slow-cooked burst of flavors, no other condiment is needed.

Active time: 1 hour | Total time: 6 hour | Serves 4–5

INGREDIENTS FOR SPICE RUB

- 1½ teaspoons black peppercorns
- 1½ teaspoons coriander seeds
- 1½ teaspoons cumin seeds
- 1½ teaspoons mustard seeds
- ½ teaspoon whole cloves
- ½ teaspoon fennel seeds
- 4 green cardamom pods
- 1 (1½-inch) cinnamon stick, broken into small pieces
- 2 tablespoons coconut flakes
- 10 to 12 whole red chilies, dry
- 1¼ teaspoons salt

INGREDIENTS FOR BEEF

- 2 pounds beef tenderloin, trimmed and chopped into thin slices of 2-inch filets
- ½ cup plain yogurt
- 1 tablespoon lemon juice
- 2 teaspoons ginger paste
- 1 teaspoon garlic paste
- 1 cup water
- 1½ tablespoons vegetable oil
- 1 medium onion, finely sliced

INGREDIENTS FOR GARNISH

- 1 red or white onion, chopped
- 1 fresh green chili, sliced and seeded
- ½ cup fresh cilantro, chopped
- 1 tablespoon ginger, finely julienned
- 1 lemon, sliced

(continued)

- Toast spices in a dry skillet over medium-low heat for 3 to 5 minutes, stirring occasionally, until mustard seeds begin to pop. Cool completely and then grind into a powder.

- In a large bowl, mix the beef, yogurt, lemon juice, ginger and garlic pastes, and spice mix. Marinate for 2 to 3 hours, or overnight for best results.

- Heat oil in a large skillet or Dutch oven over medium heat. Add onion slices and fry until caramelized. Add the marinated beef and water; mix well and cover. Cook on stove on low heat for 3 to 4 hours until meat is completely tender and juices have soaked into the meat.

- Garnish with onion, green chili, cilantro, ginger, and lemon. Serve hot with naan.

KOFTE
(Meatball Curry)

My maternal grandmother was a small, stout, and empowered lady who always dressed in a white cotton saree. She was a single mom who raised and educated her thirteen children with zest each day. She launched the first local magazine for women in her area. During this time, it was not common for women to run their own businesses. She was known for her no-nonsense attitude, kind heart, philanthropic nature, and unmatched hospitality. Her recipes were talked about across town, especially her Kofte recipe.

Active time: 30 minutes | Total time: 1 hour 15 minutes | Makes 8–10

INGREDIENTS FOR MEATBALLS

- 1 pound minced chicken or beef*
- 1 slice of bread, soaked in water for 2 minutes and then squeezed**
- 1 medium red onion, chopped roughly
- 1 teaspoon gram flour*** (besan)
- ½ cup chopped cilantro
- 1 medium jalapeno pepper, chopped roughly
- 1 teaspoon ground cumin
- ½ teaspoon ground red chili
- ½ teaspoon ground allspice
- ½ teaspoon salt
- 1 tablespoon fresh ginger, roughly chopped ****
- 1 clove garlic, chopped roughly

INGREDIENTS FOR CURRY

- ¼ cup vegetable oil
- 1 large red onion, finely sliced
- 1 teaspoon cumin seeds
- ½ teaspoon black peppercorns
- 2 whole green cardamoms
- 1 whole black cardamom
- 2 whole cloves
- 2 medium tomatoes, chopped roughly
- ½ cup plain yogurt, whisked well
- ¾ cup water, divided
- ¼ teaspoon freshly ground nutmeg
- ¼ teaspoon freshly ground mace
- ¼ teaspoon ground cinnamon
- ¼ teaspoon ground turmeric
- ½ teaspoon ground coriander
- ½ teaspoon chili powder, or to taste
- Salt, to taste
- 1 teaspoon ginger paste
- 1 teaspoon garlic paste
- ¼ cup cilantro, chopped, for garnishing

(continued)

- To make the meatballs, grind together all meatball ingredients in a food processor until everything is well blended. Put aside in the fridge for 10 to 15 minutes to bind together. With oiled hands, roll a heaped tablespoon of the mince into a medium-sized meatball; repeat until mince is gone. Set aside.

- To make the curry, heat the vegetable oil in a deep pan with a lid. Add the onion and fry on medium-low heat until light brown. Add cumin seeds, black peppercorns, green and black cardamom, and whole cloves. Fry until golden-brown.

- Place onion and spice mixture in the food processor. Add tomatoes, yogurt, and ¼ cup water, and process into a paste. In the pan with the oil, add the paste on medium-high heat and cook for 1 minute. Add the ground nutmeg, mace, cinnamon, turmeric, coriander, chili powder, salt, and ginger and garlic pastes. Sauté for 3 to 4 minutes. Add the remaining ½ cup water and mix well.

- Once curry begins to lightly bubble, add the meatballs one at a time. Gently shake the pan by lifting it and swirling it to soak the meatballs in the curry. Cover with lid and cook on medium-low for 10 to 15 minutes. Turn the heat to a simmer for 5 more minutes, then turn the stove off. The curry should be thick and the meatballs soaked. Garnish with fresh cilantro and serve over basmati rice.

---

* *Breast filets can be used instead of ground meat if chopped into cubes before mincing in the food processor*
** *Soaked bread makes the meatball melt-in-your-mouth moist*
*** *Gram flour is used for binding*
**** *Ginger is used as a tenderizer*

MURGH HARA MASALA
(Green Chicken)

These simple yet flavorful ingredients can be put together in minutes and left to cook. This recipe can be made with chicken, lamb, or chopped potatoes. The simple yet distinct flavors of the greens and spices make it taste delicious with the chutney of your choice and a side of rice or bread.

Active time: 15 minutes | *Total time: 30 minutes* | *Serves 4*

- 2 tablespoons vegetable oil
- 6 to 8 boneless chicken breasts, hammered thin*
- 1 cup cilantro, chopped
- 1 cup spring onions, chopped
- 4 green chilies, whole
- 4 garlic cloves, julienned
- 1 teaspoon fresh ginger, julienned
- ½ cup plain yogurt
- ½ teaspoon chili powder
- Salt, to taste

- Heat vegetable oil in a deep pan. Add chicken and fry for 1 to 2 minutes until slightly browned but not cooked through. Add cilantro, spring onions, green chilies, garlic cloves, ginger, yogurt, chili powder, and salt; mix well. Cover the pan and cook on medium-low heat for 10 to 15 minutes or until dry. Remove the lid and continue to cook the chicken on high heat for 2 to 3 minutes until oil is released from the sides. Serve hot with naan, pita bread, or basmati rice.

---

* *Boneless chicken cubes or whole chicken, chopped into 12 to 14 pieces, can replace chicken breasts.*

MASALA FISH

Of the hundreds of fish species available in Karachi, my father's favorite was whole pomfret, marinated with spicy masala, a Bombay-style fish that was a regular feature at our dining table at least once a week. We ate this fish as a complete meal on its own or with hot homemade rotis (flat bread) and a side of *Green Coconut Chutney*. An extra drizzle of lemon juice gives it a kick.

Active time: 15 minutes | *Total time: 45 minutes* | *Serves 2*

- 2 tablespoons salt
- 4 to 5 whole pieces of pomfret (butterfish)
- 4 tablespoons ginger paste
- 4 tablespoons garlic paste
- ½ teaspoon chili powder
- ¼ teaspoon ground turmeric
- 1 teaspoon ground cumin
- 1 teaspoon ground allspice
- 1 teaspoon ground coriander
- Salt, to taste
- 4 tablespoons fresh lemon juice
- 1 cup fresh coriander leaves, coarsely chopped
- 4 to 5 tablespoons vegetable oil

- Rub salt on the fish, and wash well. (This takes away any fishy smell). Dry well with kitchen towel.

- In a small bowl, mix ginger and garlic pastes, chili powder, turmeric, cumin, allspice, coriander, salt, lemon juice, and half of the coriander leaves to make a paste. Rub the paste on the fish and set aside to marinate in a cool place for 30 minutes.

- Heat oil in a pan to shallow-fry. Add 1 to 2 pieces of fish at a time, frying each side for 3 to 4 minutes each or until each side turns slightly crispy. Remove from pan, drain on paper towel. Garnish with the remaining coriander leaves and serve.

DAAL
(Lentil Curry)

A staple in every household in Karachi, this light curry is eaten throughout the year. This dish is a great source of nutrition for people on a diet, and can be eaten over rice or served as soup.

Active time: 15 minutes | *Total time: 1 hour* | *Serves 4–5*

FOR THE CURRY

- 1 cup split red lentils, sorted of debris and rinsed
- 2½ cups water
- 2 medium tomatoes, chopped
- 1 teaspoon fresh ginger, finely grated
- 2 garlic cloves, finely grated
- 1 teaspoon ground coriander
- 1 teaspoon chili powder, or to taste
- 1 teaspoon ground cumin
- ½ teaspoon ground allspice
- ¼ teaspoon ground turmeric
- Salt, to taste
- 2 tablespoons tamarind paste or 4 tablespoons lemon juice

FOR THE TEMPERING

- 2 to 3 tablespoons vegetable oil
- 2 garlic cloves, chopped
- 4 to 5 dried red chilies
- 1 green chili, chopped
- 1 teaspoon cumin seeds
- Fresh curry leaves

FOR THE GARNISH

- Fresh cilantro, chopped
- Lemon wedge

- In a large pot, mix lentils, water, tomatoes, ginger, garlic, coriander, chili powder, cumin, allspice, turmeric, and salt. Slow cook mixture on low heat for 30 to 45 minutes, or until the lentils are cooked, mushy, and thick. Mash the lentils with the back of a spoon or a ladle. Add the tamarind paste or lemon juice.

- For tempering, add vegetable oil in a frying pan on medium-low heat. Add garlic, red chilies, and green chili. Fry until garlic is lightly browned. Add cumin seeds and fresh curry leaves, and fry for 30 seconds. Remove from stove and pour over lentils immediately.

- Garnish with fresh chopped cilantro, squeeze some lemon on top, and serve.

SHAAMI KABAB

The preparation of Shaami Kabab was always a day-long process in my household. Once the patties were made, dozens would be stored in the freezer for several weeks at a time, first frozen as individual patties on a tray and then moved to the freezer in large resealable plastic bags. My grandmother prepared these without the use of a food processor. The meat was traditionally hand-ground on a large mortar-and-pestle-like slab. For me, the flavors that fuse together through this hands-on manual process are far earthier and more unique than the flavors that come from the machine-run process we use nowadays. These traditional slabs are still used in many households around the region.

Active time: 30 minutes | Total time: 2 hours 30 minutes | Makes 12–15

- 1 pound ground meat, such as beef or chicken
- ½ cup chana daal (split bengal gram)
- 2 medium-sized red onions, peeled and roughly chopped
- 3 to 4 garlic gloves, peeled and roughly chopped
- 1 tablespoon fresh ginger, peeled and roughly chopped
- 1 teaspoon cumin seeds
- 3 to 4 whole cloves
- 8 to 10 whole peppercorns
- 2 to 3 whole green cardamoms
- 1 to 2 whole large black cardamoms
- ½-inch stick of cinnamon
- 7 to 8 dried red chilies
- Salt, to taste
- 3 cups water
- 2 eggs, lightly beaten
- ½ cup of coriander leaves, finely chopped
- 1 medium-sized yellow onion, finely chopped
- 1 green chili, finely chopped (optional)
- ½ cup vegetable oil for frying

(continued)

- Place ground meat, chana daal, onions, garlic, ginger, cumin seeds, cloves, peppercorns, green and black cardamoms, cinnamon, red chilies, salt, and water in a large pan. Cook for about 40 minutes, or until meat and lentils are cooked and all the water is absorbed. To finish off, stir-fry on high until all the liquid is dried off and the meat looks quite dry. Allow mixture to cool. Grind in a food processor until smooth.

- In a bowl, add the meat mixture, eggs, coriander leaves, onion, and green chili. Mix well. Adjust salt if needed. Leave covered in the fridge for 2 to 24 hours for the mix to set. Divide into 12 to 15 portions and shape into a patty. Size and shape is your choice. If you are making them for a cocktail party, make them quite small.

- Heat a little oil in a non-stick frying pan. It is always a good idea to test-fry one kabab first. If it crumbles easily, add 1 to 2 tablespoons gram flour (besan) to the mix before continuing with the rest. Shallow-fry all kababs until brown and crisp on both sides. Serve hot with Green Coconut Chutney and some naan or rice.

CHICKEN CREPES

This light and savory crepe filled with a creamy chicken filling has perhaps been the most popular among my kids and their friends. This is something devoured as soon as it touches the table. For dinner parties, you can place hot crepes on individual plates and lightly drizzle with the sauce and some grated Parmesan cheese, served with a side of salad and garlic bread.

Active time: 1 hour | Total time: 1 hour 15 minutes | Makes 8

FOR THE CREPES

- 1 cup flour
- 2 cups milk
- 3 eggs
- Pinch of salt
- 3 tablespoons melted butter or vegetable oil

FOR THE WHITE SAUCE

- 3 tablespoons butter
- 3 tablespoons flour
- 1½ cups milk
- Salt, to taste
- Pepper, to taste
- ½ teaspoon chili flakes
- ½ cup cream
- 4 tablespoons soy sauce

FOR THE FILLING

- 2 cups cooked and shredded chicken breast
- 4 tablespoons butter
- 1 teaspoon garlic paste
- ½ teaspoon chili flakes
- Salt, to taste
- ½ teaspoon ground black pepper
- 1 cup mushrooms, chopped
- 1 cup sweet corn
- 3 cups white sauce, recipe above
- 1 cup grated cheddar cheese

CREPES

- Mix all the ingredients with a whisk. Heat pan, pour batter into center of pan, and swirl pan until bottom is covered with a thin layer of batter. Flip crepe and cook the second side. The first side will be a nice, even brown; the second side will be an uneven color. When both sides are cooked,

(continued)

remove from pan, spread finished crepes out, and allow to dry before stacking. If you make ahead and freeze, stack between pieces of wax paper.

WHITE SAUCE

- Melt butter in a pan. Stir in the flour and cook for 1 to 2 minutes on medium-low, stirring constantly with a whisk or wooden spoon (don't let mixture brown). Take the pan off the heat and gradually stir in the milk, constantly stirring to get a smooth sauce. Return to heat and simmer 8 to 10 minutes, stirring to prevent scorching. Add salt, pepper, and chili flakes. Add cream bit by bit and mix well. As the sauce will thicken with baking, make sure the sauce has a thinner consistency. If sauce is too thick, add milk until you get a thinner consistency. Add soy sauce and mix well.

FILLING

- Preheat oven to 375°F/190°C. Heat butter in skillet until bubbling. Cook onions for 1 to 2 minutes. Add chili flakes, salt, and pepper. Add mushrooms and cook until they are slightly browned and soft. Add corn and chicken and combine with pan juices. Add half a cup of white sauce to chicken and mix well.

- Fill each crepe with chicken filling, roll and turn seam side down in a buttered baking dish. Top with the remaining white sauce and cheese and bake for 20 minutes. The filling can be frozen for up to 2 weeks without the sauce and cheese.

KAUSARI RICE

Having been a working mother of three children, I was always looking to create nutritious recipes that were not time-consuming and that my children liked. Making children eat vegetables is probably the most difficult task at times, but this vegetarian rice dish is a sure winner! I created this recipe with vegetables that are available all year round, a sauce that comes together in minutes, and a topping of nuts and fried garlic. A dear friend named it "Kausari Rice." I have always made this as a vegetarian dish, but for meat lovers, cubed and boiled chicken can be added to the vegetable mixture.

Active time: 20 minutes | *Total time: 40 minutes* | *Serves 6*

FOR THE RICE

3 cups rice

1 cup cabbage, finely chopped

1 cup carrot, finely julienned

1 cup red pepper, finely julienned

1 cup green onions, chopped lengthwise

1 cup mayonnaise

½ cup ketchup

1 teaspoon soy sauce

¼ teaspoon crushed red pepper (optional)

Salt, to taste

Pepper, to taste

FOR THE GARNISH

10 garlic cloves, sliced and fried on medium-low heat until golden-brown

1 cup roasted, salted peanuts or roasted cashews

- Boil rice and set aside. In a deep pan, on medium heat, add cabbage, carrot, capsicum, and green onions. Add mayonnaise, ketchup, soy sauce, crushed red pepper (optional), salt, and pepper, and cook on medium-low heat for 5 to 8 minutes until well mixed and hot (do not overcook). Let the vegetables remain crispy. Just before serving, place hot rice in serving platter and top with the vegetables and sauce. Garnish with fried garlic and peanuts or cashews.

MUTTON DO PYAZA
(Lamb Stew)

Mutton Do Pyaza (Lamb Stew) is a South Asian stew with a history that can be traced back to the Mughal empire. This simple recipe for *Mutton Do Pyaza* can be made with chicken, lamb, or goat meat mixed with spices, and is traditionally served with naan and a side of Raita or plain yogurt.

Active time: 15 minutes | **Total time:** 1 hour 15 minutes | **Serves** 2–3

- 3 tablespoons vegetable oil
- 1¼ pounds goat or lamb meat, cut into chunks with bones (leg meat works well here, as it cooks up tender)
- 6 to 7 small red onions, finely sliced
- 1 large tomato, chopped
- 5 to 6 garlic cloves, finely sliced
- 1 tablespoon fresh ginger, finely sliced
- 4 to 5 whole dried red chilies
- ¼ teaspoon cumin seeds
- 6 to 7 whole black peppercorns
- 4 to 5 whole cloves
- 2 to 3 whole green cardamoms
- 2 to 3 whole large black cardamoms
- 1 (2½-inch) cinnamon stick
- Salt, to taste
- ½ cup plain yogurt
- 1 cup water

FOR THE GARNISH
- ¼ cup fresh coriander, chopped
- 2 green chilies, sliced lengthwise

- In a deep pan, heat the oil over medium heat and add the meat. Stir fry for 2 to 3 minutes. Add the red onions, tomato, garlic, ginger, red chilies, cumin seeds, peppercorns, cloves, green and black cardamoms, cinnamon stick, salt, yogurt, and water; mix well. Cover the pan and let cook for 50 to 60 minutes on medium-low heat, or until meat is tender and water is absorbed. Uncover and stir-fry on medium-low for 4 to 5 minutes or until oil is released. There should be a thick gravy sauce. Transfer meat and sauce to a serving dish. Garnish with chopped coriander and green chilies. Serve with hot naan and a side of Raita or plain yogurt

LENTIL *and* RICE PILAF

One of my favorite childhood dishes was the meatless *Lentil and Rice Pilaf* my mom made, topped with sliced boiled eggs and garnished with fried onion, fresh green chili, and cilantro. I feel nostalgic each time I cook this dish. While playing outside our house with my brothers on a late Sunday morning, I could smell the spices with a touch of saffron, and I instantly knew what was cooking. Pakistanis are well-known meat lovers, but I love vegetarian recipes like this one the most.

Active time: 40 minutes | Total time: 1 hour 10 minutes | Serves 4

FOR THE PILAF

- ¼ cup vegetable oil
- 1 cup yellow onion, finely chopped
- 1 clove garlic, minced
- 1 teaspoon ginger, minced
- 1 cup split black gram (kaali daal), sorted of debris and rinsed
- 1 teaspoon salt
- ¾ teaspoon ground cumin
- ½ teaspoon chili powder
- ¼ teaspoon turmeric
- ½ teaspoon ground coriander
- ½ teaspoon ground allspice
- ¾ cup long-grain white basmati rice
- 2 cups water
- ¼ teaspoon saffron, soaked in 1 teaspoon milk

FOR THE GARNISH

- 2 eggs, hardboiled and sliced
- 1 medium onion, finely sliced and fried brown and crispy
- ¼ cup cilantro, chopped
- 2 green chilies, sliced lengthwise
- Raita yogurt sauce

- Heat vegetable oil in a large pan and add onions. Fry over medium heat; stir often until onions are golden-brown. Add ginger and garlic. Add water, split black gram (kaali daal), salt, cumin, chili powder, turmeric,

(continued)

coriander, and allspice. Cover and let it cook for 20 to 25 minutes on medium heat until lentils are half-tender to bite.

- Stir in the basmati rice and 2 more cups water. Bring to a boil over high heat; reduce heat and simmer, gently stirring from sides, until rice is tender to bite and liquid is absorbed (13 to 15 minutes). Add the saffron with milk. Cover, let simmer for 10 minutes. Garnish with sliced hardboiled eggs, fried onion, cilantro, and green chilies, and serve with *Raita*.

KHAO SUEY
(Coconut Noodle Soup)

This Burmese dish is a perfect combination of thick coconut soup and fragrant chicken poured over soft noodles, garnished with crunchy fried spaghetti, fiery chilies, boiled egg, lemon juice, and aromatic coriander. This recipe was introduced to me through a Burmese family friend. Later, I discovered a variety of versions through friends and family.

Active time: 1 hour 30 minutes | *Total time: 1 hour 30 minutes* | *Serves 5–6*

FOR THE CHICKEN

2 to 3 chicken breasts, cut into small cubes

1 teaspoon garlic paste

1 teaspoon chili powder

Salt, to taste

2 to 3 tablespoons of vegetable oil for frying

FOR THE SOUP

2 cups coconut milk

2 cups coconut powder

2 cups water

1 tablespoon gram flour mixed in ¼ cup water*

1 teaspoon garlic paste

1 teaspoon chili powder

1 teaspoon salt

½ teaspoon ground turmeric

16 ounces spaghetti noodles, boiled and drained

FOR THE GARNISH

2 tablespoons vegetable oil, divided

1 cup uncooked spaghetti, broken into small 1-inch long pieces

2 spring onions, chopped finely

6 garlic cloves, chopped

2 eggs, hardboiled and sliced

½ cup of coriander, chopped

½ cup of mint leaves

2 lemons, quartered

2 red onions, finely sliced and fried crisp

Chili oil (optional—for spicier Khao Suey)

(continued)

---

*Gram flour is used to thicken the soup. If you cannot find gram flour, allow soup to cook for an extra 10 minutes until it has cooked down to a thicker consistency.

CHICKEN *and* SOUP

- Place the cubed chicken in a bowl and add the garlic paste, chili powder, and salt. Mix well to coat the chicken evenly. Heat oil in a pan and add the marinated chicken. Cook chicken until there is no pink in the middle and juices run clear. Set aside.

- In a large pot, add the soup ingredients and let it simmer on medium-low heat for 45 minutes, stirring the mixture after every 5 minutes. After 45 minutes, try the soup to see if you can taste the flour. If not, your soup is ready. My Khao Suey recipe is soupy; let it cook for longer to get it down to a thicker curry consistency.

GARNISH

- Heat 1 tablespoon of oil in a pan. Break the uncooked spaghetti into small pieces and fry in the oil until they are crisp and light brown. Soak on a kitchen towel to remove the excess oil. Fry onion and garlic separately with 1 tablespoon of vegetable oil over medium heat for 3 to 5 minutes, until onion begins to become translucent. Drain on a kitchen towel and set aside.

- Place all the garnish ingredients on a platter, separated.

- To serve, mix soup with cooked noodles and chicken, then top with garnishes, one at a time. For a spicier version, pour some chili oil over the Khao Suey.

DESSERTS

NAN KHATAI
(Shortbread Biscuit)

These biscuits were traditionally baked in clay ovens. They are an all-time favorite teatime biscuit, commonly dunked in tea, which gives them that soft melt-in-the-mouth effect. The addition of semolina gives these biscuits a special crunch.

Active time: 25 minutes | *Total time: 40 minutes* | *Makes 10–12*

- 1 cup flour
- 2 tablespoons semolina
- ¼ teaspoon baking soda
- ¼ teaspoon ground cardamom
- Pinch of salt
- ½ cup unsalted butter, room temperature
- ½ cup granulated sugar
- 1 tablespoon pistachios, finely chopped

- Preheat oven to 350°F/180°C. Sieve flour in a bowl; add semolina, baking soda, cardamom, and salt, and combine. In another bowl, whisk together butter and sugar until smooth and fluffy. Add flour mixture. Using your hands, mix wet and dry ingredients into medium-soft dough.

- Line a cookie sheet with parchment paper. Divide dough into 18 equal portions and make into balls. (If dough is very soft, refrigerate for 10 to 15 minutes before shaping balls.) Take each ball and press a little between your palms to give it a patty-like shape; place the balls on the cookie sheet. Top each cookie with a little bit of pistachios and press gently with your finger. Keep enough space between each biscuit; they will expand in size during baking. Bake for 15 to 18 minutes, or until biscuits start to turn light-golden in color. Remove baking tray from oven, transfer biscuits to a wire rack, and let them cool. Transfer them to an airtight container for storage.

FRUIT TRIFLE

I become nostalgic each time I make this dessert, revisiting memories from my childhood and motherhood. This is a favorite treat in summertime, when a large variety of fresh fruit is available. The most common fruit dishes available in Karachi during the summer are fresh fruit salads sold on carts as street food and fresh fruit trifles made in homes. Making this dish was a great way to get my kids to eat fruit. For me, bananas are always a must-add.

Active time: 45 minutes | *Total time: 45 minutes* | *Serves 8–10*

FOR THE CUSTARD

2½ cups milk

5 tablespoons sugar

2 tablespoons custard powder

3 tablespoons milk, warmed

FOR THE TRIFLE

1 packet strawberry gelatin dessert (or a gelatin dessert of your choice)

Fresh seasonal fruit, sliced into bite-sized pieces

Nuts of your choice (optional)

2 cups whipped cream

1 pound sponge cake (recipe for *Black Forest Cake* can be used here), sliced in 2-inch slices

2 cups custard

CUSTARD

- In a thick-bottomed pan, bring the 2½ cups of milk to a gentle simmer on low heat. When the milk is warm, add sugar. Stir well so that the sugar dissolves. In a bowl, add the 3 tablespoons warm milk and the custard powder, and whisk together to make a smooth custard paste without any lumps. Gradually add the custard paste to the milk and sugar in the pan. Cook for about 5 to 6 minutes, constantly stirring, until slightly thick. Set aside. Allow the custard to cool at room temperature, keeping in mind that as the custard cools, it will thicken more.

(continued)

TRIFLE

- Make the gelatin dessert according to instructions. Set aside. Start layering the trifle by starting with the strawberry gelatin dessert at the bottom. Follow with sliced fruit (and nuts if using). Add a layer with whipped cream. Follow with the cake and then the custard. Repeat the layers again in the same order. Top it off with the whipped cream topping and arrange sliced fresh fruit on top. Your trifle is ready. Keep it in the refrigerator overnight and serve chilled!

GAJAR KA HALWA
(Carrot Delight)

Gajar Ka Halwa is a dense traditional Pakistani dessert served at festive occasions. Even with the relatively small list of ingredients, every household has a different way of making this dish. This is a family recipe that was passed down to my mother by her grandmother.

Active time: 1 hour 10 minutes | *Total time:* 2 hours | *Serves 6*

- 10 to 12 almonds
- 10 to 12 unsalted pistachios, shell removed
- 1½ cups hot water
- 8 to 9 medium carrots
- 4 cups whole milk
- 4 tablespoons ghee, vegetable oil, or unsalted butter
- 5 to 6 whole green cardamoms
- 5 to 6 whole cloves
- 10 to 12 tablespoons white sugar, to taste
- Pinch of saffron
- ¼ cup of golden raisins

- Soak the almonds and pistachios in hot water for 5 minutes. Peel and finely slice the nuts and keep aside. Rinse, peel, and grate the carrots, either with a handheld grater or in a food processor.

- In a deep, heavy-based pot, add all of the grated carrots with the whole milk. Stir the grated carrots and milk, and keep the pot on the stovetop. Cook this mixture on medium-low heat. The milk will froth and start reducing gradually. Keep on stirring the mixture often. Keep scraping the sides of the pot to remove the evaporated milk solids, adding them back to the mixture. The mixture should reduce by 75 percent. Cook for around 50 minutes.

(continued)

- In another pot, heat ghee, oil, or butter on low heat. Add cardamoms and cloves and fry for 15 seconds. Add the carrot mixture and sugar. Mix well and continue to simmer on low heat until the mixture starts to thicken and reduce. Keep stirring at intervals to make sure it does not stick to the pan. Stir-fry the mixture on medium-low heat until it releases butter. Add saffron. Remove from heat and add the raisins, almonds, and pistachios. Serve hot or cold with whipped cream or coconut cream.

PINEAPPLE SOUFFLÉ

Made of cool ingredients for a hot summer day, this combination of pineapple, cream, and gelatin creates a mouthwatering dessert. You can serve this treat in a large dessert bowl or individual parfait glasses. This dish tastes best when chilled in the freezer, and then kept in the fridge to thaw one hour before serving. The texture will be like ice cream. This can be made a week in advance and frozen.

Active time: 15 minutes | *Total time: 1 hour 15 minutes* | *Serves 6–8*

- 1 15-ounce can pineapple chunks
- Sugar, to taste (optional)
- 1 packet pineapple gelatin dessert
- 1 12-ounce can evaporated milk
- 1 cup heavy whipped cream

- Separate the pineapple chunks and pineapple juice. Divide pineapple chunks in two equal portions. Finely chop half the pineapple chunks and place in a bowl. Place the remaining pineapple chunks in the blender and pulse until pineapple is finely minced. Add sugar to sweeten if desired.

- Place the pineapple juice in a pan and heat on low until juice is warm. Remove from stove and add the pineapple gelatin dessert packet, stirring well.

- Pour the gelatin mixture into the blender with the pulsed pineapple. Add the whipped cream and evaporated milk and blend well. Pour into a dessert bowl, add the finely chopped pineapple, and mix well. Cover the bowl with a plastic wrap and freeze for at least 1 hour. If frozen overnight, place it in the fridge 1 hour before serving.

VANILLA SAFFRON CHEESECAKE

This cheesecake recipe brings back one of my favorite motherhood memories, as this dessert was one of my kids' favorites. Cheesecakes come in dozens of flavors and textures. Contrasting with the dense, baked cheesecakes, this frozen version with a touch of saffron comes with a light and unique flavor.

Active time: 1 hour | Total time: 5 hours | Serves: 10

FOR THE CRUST
- 6 tablespoons unsalted butter
- 1½ cups graham crackers, finely crushed
- 2 tablespoons sugar

FOR THE FILLING
- 1 tablespoon unflavored gelatin
- ¼ cup water, warmed
- 3 eggs, separated
- ¼ cup sugar
- ½ teaspoon salt
- 2 tablespoons saffron
- 2 tablespoons lemon juice
- 1 teaspoon lemon zest
- 2 cups cream cheese
- ½ cup white sugar, granulated

CRUST

- Preheat the oven to 350°F/180°C. Place the butter in a medium bowl and melt, covered, in the microwave. Grease a 9-inch spring form pan with some of the butter. Stir the remaining butter together with the graham crumbs and sugar. Press the crumb mixture over the bottom of the pan, taking care to get the crust evenly into the edges. Bake about 15 minutes until golden-brown; set aside to cool.

(continued)

DIRECTIONS FOR FILLING

- In a small bowl, add 1 tablespoon of gelatin in warm water and set aside. Beat egg yolks. Place a double boiler with the bowl placed on top of a pan, ¼ full of simmering water, on low heat; make sure the bowl does not touch the water in the pan beneath. Combine egg yolks, sugar, salt, saffron, lemon juice, and lemon zest; add to double boiler, whisking constantly to avoid lumps. Cook until the mixture is thick and creamy, about 3 minutes.

- Remove from heat and add the softened gelatin, stirring until dissolved. Let mixture cool completely. In a bowl, lightly combine cream cheese and sugar. Mix with the cooled egg yolk mixture. In a clean and dry bowl, beat three egg whites until soft peaks form. Fold the beaten egg whites gently into the cream cheese mixture. Spread over the crust and chill for at least 4 to 5 hours, or until set and chilled.

APPLE PIE

The aroma of apple pie conjures warmth, taste, and togetherness. This pie is filled with juicy apples tucked into a buttery crust with a touch of cinnamon, which enriches the aroma and taste buds. I love the idea of individual, mini apple pies, which I often made in mini pie pans. The pie dough may be made a day ahead and refrigerated or wrapped in plastic and frozen for up to a month.

Active time: 1 hour 30 minutes | Total time: 2 hours 30 minutes | Serves: 6–8

FOR THE PÂTE BRISÉE (PIE CRUST DOUGH)

- 1½ cups flour
- ½ teaspoon salt
- ½ teaspoon sugar
- ½ cup unsalted butter, chilled and cut in pieces
- ¼ to ½ cup ice water

FOR THE PIE FILLING

- 12 Granny Smith apples, peeled, cored, and sliced
- ¾ cup sugar, plus additional for pie top
- 1 lemon, juiced and zested
- 1½ teaspoons ground cinnamon
- 2 tablespoons flour
- 2 tablespoons unsalted butter
- 1 large egg, beaten

PÂTE BRISÉE (PIE CRUST DOUGH)

- Place the flour, salt, and sugar in the bowl of a food processor (the same can be done by hand in a bowl) and process for a few seconds to combine. Add the chilled butter and process until the mixture resembles coarse meal, about 10 seconds. With the machine running, add the ice water in a slow, steady stream, through the feed tube, just until the dough holds together. Do not process for more than 30 seconds.

(continued)

- Turn the dough out onto a work surface. Place the dough on a sheet of plastic wrap. Flatten and form into a disc. Wrap and refrigerate for at least 1 hour before using.

PIE

- Heat oven to 375°F/190°C. On a lightly floured surface, roll out pâte brisée into a ⅛-inch thick circle with a diameter slightly larger than that of an 11-inch plate.

- In a large bowl, combine apples, sugar, lemon juice, lemon zest, cinnamon, and flour. Toss well. Spoon apples into pie pan. Dot with butter and cover with pâte brisée circle. Cut several steam vents across top. Seal by crimping edges as desired. Brush with beaten egg and sprinkle with additional sugar. Bake on the top rack for 1 hour, or until crust is golden-brown and juices are bubbling. Let cool on wire rack before serving. Serve with whipped cream.

BLACK FOREST CAKE

When I was in my teens, there was only one bakery in Karachi that served this delicious German cake. Baking was rarely done at home, as ovens were uncommon. My mom created her very own concoction of *Black Forest Cake*, and until we got our own oven, she would send it to the neighborhood *naan* (bread) shop to get it baked in their tandoor-clay oven. I remember my mother making a very light sponge, and this is what I am sharing with you. Originally cherries were used in the recipe, but as I remember my mother using peaches, that is exactly what I do.

Active time: 1 hour 30 minutes | *Total time: 2 hours* | *Serves 10–12*

FOR THE CAKE

- ½ cup flour
- 1½ teaspoon baking powder
- ¼ cup cocoa powder
- ¼ teaspoon salt
- ½ cup milk
- 3 eggs
- ¾ cup sugar
- 1 teaspoon vanilla extract
- 3 tablespoons unsalted butter, melted and cooled, plus more for buttering cake pan

FOR THE FILLING

- 1 cup sugar
- ¼ cup cornstarch
- 2 cups peeled and sliced fresh peaches*
- 3 cups heavy whipping cream
- ⅓ cup confectioners' sugar

CAKE

- Preheat the oven to 350°F/180°C. Sift flour with baking powder, cocoa powder, and salt; set aside. Heat the milk in a small pan on low heat until

(continued)

---

* *Canned peaches can be used if fresh are not in season.*

bubbling at edge; set aside. In a small bowl, beat eggs at high speed, until thick and lemon-colored. Gradually add sugar, beating until mixture is smooth and well blended, about 5 minutes. Add vanilla extract, warm milk, and melted butter, blend until smooth. Immediately pour batter into ungreased, 9-inch cake pan. Bake 30 minutes, or until a toothpick comes out clean. Remove from the oven and let cool.

FILLING

- In a small saucepan, whisk together sugar and cornstarch; add peaches. Cook and stir over low heat for 10 to 12 minutes or until thickened and bubbly. Remove from heat; cool completely. In a large bowl, beat heavy whipping cream until it begins to thicken. Add confectioners' sugar; beat until stiff peaks form.

- Using a long serrated knife, cut cake horizontally in half. Place one cake layer on a serving plate. Top with 1½ cups whipped cream. Spread ¾ cup peaches. Top with remaining cake layer.

- Frost top and sides of cake with remaining whipped cream, reserving some to pipe decorations, if desired. Spoon remaining peaches on top of cake. Refrigerate until serving.

SHAHI TUKRAY
(Bread Pudding)

This decadent *Shahi Tukray* recipe has a history that goes back to royal Mughal kitchens. It is a delectable dessert that combines the aromas of cardamom, saffron, and rosewater with the sweetness of sugar and the richness of milk and cream. Almonds, pistachios, and raisins make this into a rich dessert fit for the kings! Serve it warm with whipped cream or coconut cream.

Active time: 30 minutes | *Total time:* 60 minutes | *Serves 10*

- 2¼ cups milk
- ½ cup cream
- 1 cup sugar
- 2 tablespoons rosewater*
- 10 slices of fresh bread (white or brown)
- 4 to 6 tablespoons vegetable oil or butter for frying bread slices
- ½ teaspoon ground cardamom
- 8 to 10 blanched almonds, finely sliced
- 8 to 10 blanched pistachios, finely sliced
- 2 tablespoons raisins

- Preheat the oven to 350°F/180°C. Boil milk, cream, and sugar in a deep-bottom pan on medium heat. Condense the milk until it becomes half in quantity, and is thick and creamy. Keep stirring occasionally to keep it from sticking to the bottom. Once milk is condensed, turn off the heat and add rosewater. Set aside.

(continued)

---

* *Rosewater can be found in most Middle Eastern and South Asian grocery stores.*

- Cut the bread slices diagonally into two. Heat oil in a skillet and shallow-fry the bread slices on both sides until golden-brown. Arrange the bread slices in a greased 9 × 12-inch baking dish.

- Pour the creamy rosewater mixture evenly over the bread slices. Sprinkle with cardamom, almonds, pistachios, and raisins. Set aside for 5 minutes to allow bread to soak.

- Cover the dish with aluminum foil and bake for 25 to 30 minutes, or until the liquid is almost evaporated and sauce has thickened. Remove from oven and set aside for 5 minutes without removing the foil. Serve hot.

ACKNOWLEDGMENTS

I would like to express my gratitude to the very special people in my life who made it possible for this book to get published.

To Sadaf, my oldest daughter, without whom this book would not exist. You pushed me to compile the recipes and helped get the book together. Zain, thank you for tasting all the food, making endless trips to the grocery store, and letting me turn your home into a studio. Sidra, your support in the pursuit of this project has been phenomenal. Your energy and encouragement have pushed me forward with confidence. Scott and Haamid, thank you for your encouragement and your inspiring love for food. Farah Ahed of Farah Ahed Photography, thank you for always being a phone call away and, as always, for the beautiful portraits. Maryam Ashraf of Marsha Photography, you are a true friend. Thank you for the great last-minute photographs.

Thank you to my parents for their love and support. My mother tasted each recipe, provided suggestions, and of course, approved each recipe in this book. My father may not be with me, but his presence is strongly felt.

A very special thank you to Williams Sonoma for providing the culinary props, tools, and accessories for the photography in this cookbook.

To my team—Amy of Wise Ink Creative Publishing, Joyce, and David—this book would have been impossible without you. Thank you for your hard work, attention to detail, and technical and creative mastery.

I would like to thank my family and friends who have supported me through my culinary journey over the years. The list is too long to name here but you know who you are. I wouldn't be here without you.

ABOUT THE AUTHOR

Born in Karachi, Pakistan, Kausar Ahmed is a food stylist, chef, and cooking instructor with over 20 years of experience in culinary arts. *The Karachi Kitchen* is her debut cookbook and features the author's favorite recipes from the crossroads of South Asia.

Kausar's love for cooking started at family meals and eventually evolved into a career. Growing up in a big Pakistani family, it was easy for Kausar to be enamored with food from a young age. *"Warm smells would float out of the kitchen and cause a sensory explosion,"* she says about her mother's fresh, home-cooked meals, where ingredients like turmeric, cumin, and ginger were frequently used, along with whatever else happened to be in season. As she started helping her mother in the kitchen, cooking became a therapeutic activity—bringing people together over a meal gave her immense pleasure as it brought her community closer together.

Being raised in Karachi played an important role in Kausar's evolution, as her passion became a career. Regional cuisine in Karachi is a hybrid of Asian, European, and Middle Eastern ingredients and styles of preparation. The city is a trade hub that sits where South Asia collides.

"Karachi is a dynamic, multi-lingual city extremely rich in culinary and cultural history. It is the most ethnically diverse city in the country and one of the most populated in the world. Local food is bold in flavor, and comes in many forms including curries, soups, stews, wraps, pilafs, pies, and more. For The Karachi Kitchen *I have compiled some of my favorites: recipes deeply connected to my own childhood, and others connected to motherhood. I hope they bring my readers as much curiosity and adventure as they brought me when I first discovered them."*

Since her foray into culinary arts Kausar has served as a chef, food stylist, cooking show producer and host, and culinary instructor in Pakistan and the United States. The internationally-acclaimed entrepreneur has worked with top global brands such as Unilever, Nestlé, Williams Sonoma, and more.

Kausar is best known for her work through "Kitchen Craft," an organization she founded in 2009 that offers free nutrition and cooking workshops to women and youth in high-risk communities around Karachi, with the goal of promoting healthy eating and hygiene habits amongst impoverished families. Hands-on workshops teach students about cooking, nutrition, kitchen safety, personal hygiene, gardening, and more. Workshops for children are focused on improving language, reading, motor, memory, and interpersonal skills.

Kausar is a member of the International Association of Culinary Professionals and currently works as a freelance food consultant, stylist, and educator. She is working on her next cookbook and spends her time between Karachi and California.

Get in touch with Kausar at **thekarachikitchen@gmail.com**. Learn more about Kausar at **kausarahmed.net**.

INDEX

NOTE: Page numbers in italics indicate photographs while page numbers with *n* indicate footnotes.

A

Aaloo Chaat (Potato Salad), 4, 7, *16*, 17
Achar (Carrot Pickle), *12*, 13
Apple Pie, 75, *76*, 77
Asafetida powder, 13*n*

B

Beef
    Dum Kay Pasanday (Masala-Rubbed Roast Beef Tenderloin), *32*, 33–34
    Kofte (Meatball Curry), 35, *36*, 37
Biscuit, Nan Khatai, *62*, 63
Black Forest Cake, *78*, 79–80
Bread, Rotis, 41
Bread Pudding, Shahi Tukray, 81, *82*, 83
Bun Kabab with Green Coconut Chutney (Traditional Potato Burger), *22*, 23

C

Cake
    Black Forest Cake, *78*, 79–80
    Vanilla Saffron Cheesecake, *72*, 73–74
Chaat Masala, 7*n*, 27*n*

Chicken
    breasts, cubes, whole, 37*n*
    Khao Suey (Coconut Noodle Soup), 57, *58*, 59
    Murgh Hara Masala (Green Chicken), *38*, 39
    Mutton Do Pyaza (Lamb Stew), *52*, 53
Chicken Crepes, 47, *48*, 49
Chips, Fried Okra, *14*, 15
Chutney
    Bun Kabab with Green Coconut Chutney (Traditional Potato Burger), *22*, 23
    Green Coconut Chutney, *1*, 5, *22*, 23, 29, 41
    Sweet and Spicy Plum Chutney, 2, *3*
    Tamarind and Date Chutney, *6*, 7, 25
    Tamarind and Mint Chutney, 5
Crust
    Apple Pie, 75
    Vanilla Saffron Cheesecake, *72*, 73–74
Curry
    Daal (Lentil Curry), *42*, 43
    Kofte (Meatball Curry), 35, *36*, 37
    where to find leaves, 25*n*
Custard, Fruit Trifle, *64*, 65–66

D

Daal (Lentil Curry), *42*, 43

Dahi Bare (Dumplings in Yogurt), 4, 7, *24*, 25–26
Desserts
    Apple Pie, 75, *76*, 77
    Black Forest Cake, *78*, 79–80
    Fruit Trifle, *64*, 65–66
    Gajar Ka Halwa (Carrot Delight), 67, *68*, 69
    Nan Khatai (Shortbread Biscuit), *62*, 63
    Pineapple Soufflé, *70*, 71
    Shahi Tukray (Bread Pudding), 81, *82*, 83
    Vanilla Saffron Cheesecake, 72, 73–74
Dum Kay Pasanday (Masala-Rubbed Roast Beef Tenderloin), *32*, 33–34
Dumplings, Dahi Bare, 4, 7, *24*, 25–26

F

Fish, Masala, 2, 21, *40*, 41
Fried Okra Chips, *14*, 15
Fritters, Stuffed Green Pepper Pakoras, 27, *28*, 29
Fruit Trifle, *64*, 65–66

G

Gajar Ka Halwa (Carrot Delight), 67, *68*, 69
Ginger, 37*n*
Goat, Mutton Do Pyaza (Lamb Stew), *52*, 53
Gram flour, 37*n*, 57*n*
Green Coconut Chutney, *1*, 2, 22, 23, 29, 45

J

Jaggery, 7*n*

K

Kabab
    Bun Kabab with Green Coconut Chutney (Traditional Potato Burger), *22*, 23
    Shaami Kabab, 1, 21, *44*, 45
Kausari Rice, *50*, 51
Khao Suey (Coconut Noodle Soup), 57, *58*, 69
Kofte (Meatball Curry), 35, *36*, 37

L

Lamb, Mutton Do Pyaza (Stew), *52*, 53
Lentil and Rice Pilaf, 1, 2, 27, *54*, 55–56
Lentil Curry, *42*, 43

M

Main courses
    Chicken Crepes, 47, *48*, 49
    Daal (Lentil Curry), *42*, 43
    Dum Kay Pasanday (Masala-Rubbed Roast Beef Tenderloin), *32*, 33–34
    Kausari Rice, *50*, 51
    Khao Suey (Coconut Noodle Soup), 57, *58*, 59
    Kofte (Meatball Curry), 35, *36*, 37
    Lentil and Rice Pilaf, 1, 2, 27, *54*, 55–56
    Masala Fish, 2, 21, *40*, 41

Murgh Hara Masala (Green Chicken), *38*, 39
Mutton Do Pyaza (Lamb Stew), *52*, 53
Shaami Kabab, 1, 21, *44*, 45
Masala
   Chaat Masala, 7*n*, 27*n*
   Dum Kay Pasanday (Masala-Rubbed Roast Beef Tenderloin), *32*, 33–34
   Murgh Hara Masala (Green Chicken), *38*, 39
Masala Fish, 2, 21, *40*, 41
Masala Spice Blend, 4
Murgh Hara Masala (Green Chicken), *38*, 39
Mutton Do Pyaza (Lamb Stew), *52*, 53

N
Namak Paray (Pastry Ribbons), *18*, 19
Nan Khatai (Shortbread Biscuit), *62*, 63

P
Papri, 25
Pie, Apple, 75, *76*, 77
Pilaf, Lentil and Rice, 1, 2, 27, *54*, 55–56
Pineapple Soufflé, *70*, 71
Potato Burger, *22*, 23
Potato Salad. see Aaloo Chaat (Potato Salad)

R
Raita (Yogurt Sauce), 8, *9*, 27, 53, 56
Rice
   Kausari Rice, *50*, 51
   Lentil and Rice Pilaf, 1, 2, 27, *54*, 55–56
Rosewater, 81*n*
Rotis (Flat Bread), 41

S
Salad
   Potato Salad (see Aaloo Chat)
   Spiced Orange Salad, *20*, 21
Sauces. see Toppings and sauces
Shaami Kabab, 1, 25, *44*, 45
Shahi Tukray (Bread Pudding), 81, *82*, 83
Sides and Snacks
   Aaloo Chaat (Potato Salad), 4, 7, *16*, 17
   Achar (Carrot Pickle), *12*, 13
   Bun Kabab with Green Coconut Chutney (Traditional Potato Burger), *22*, 23
   Dahi Bare (Dumplings in Yogurt), 4, 7, *24*, 25–26
   Fried Okra Chips, *14*, 15
   Namak Paray (Pastry Ribbons), *17*, 19
   Spiced Orange Salad, 4, *20*, 21
   Stuffed Green Pepper Pakoras (Fritters), 27, *28*, 29
Soufflé, Pineapple, *70*, 71
Spice Blend, Masala, 4
Spiced Orange Salad, 4, *20*, 21
Stew and Soup
   Khao Suey (Coconut Noodle Soup), 57, *58*, 59
   Mutton Do Pyaza (Lamb Stew), *52*, 53

Stuffed Green Pepper Pakoras (Fritters), 27, *28*, 29
Sweet and Spicy Plum Chutney, 2, *3*

T

Tamarind and Date Chutney, *6*, 7, 25
Tamarind and Mint Chutney, 5
Toppings and sauces
    Green Coconut Chutney, 1, *22*, 23, 29, 41
    Masala Spice Blend, 4
    Raita (Yogurt Sauce), 8, *19*, 27, 53, 56
    Sweet and Spicy Plum Chutney, 2, *3*
    Tamarind and Date Chutney, *6*, 7, 25
    Tamarind and Mint Chutney, 5
Trifle, Fruit, *64*, 65–66

V

Vanilla Saffron Cheesecake, *72*, 73–74

Y

Yogurt
    Dahi Bare (Dumplings in Yogurt), 4, 7, *24*, 25–26
    Mutton Do Pyaza (Lamb Stew), *52*, 53
    Raita (Yogurt Sauce), *8*, 9, 27, 53, 56